Look and See

written by Anne Giulieri
illustrated by Cherie Zamazing

Look at the *jungle*.
Can you see all the *animals*?
They are hiding in the jungle.

Can you find an ant?
Can you find a *giraffe* too?

Look at the *clouds*.
They are white and *fluffy*.

Look at the clouds again.
Can you see all the animals?

Can you find an *elephant*?
Can you find a cat too?

Look at the *wall*.

Can you see a dog?

It is a *shadow* of a dog.

The shadow is made
with your *hands* and *light*.

Can you make a dog shadow
with your hands?

Can you make lots of shadows
with your hands?

Look at the girl and boy.
They are playing on the *beach*.

Can you see the boy's legs?

You cannot see the boy's legs. They are hiding in the sand.

Look at the *sandbox*.
Can you see the *toys*?
They are hiding in the sandbox.

Look at the *picture*.

Can you see 2 animals?

Have a good look.

Can you see a duck?

Can you see a rabbit too?

Picture Glossary

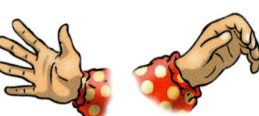
hands

sandbox

animals

elephant

jungle

shadow

beach

fluffy

light

toys

clouds

giraffe

picture

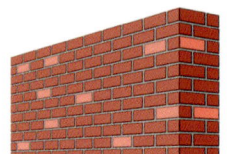
wall